THE LUCKLESS MONSTER

Michaela Morgan

Illustrated by Martina Selway

OXFORD
UNIVERSITY PRESS

1

Monsters

Do you think you know all about monsters?

You've probably heard of the Big Bad Troll. He was famous for frightening goats.

You've probably heard of the deadly dragon. It was famous for fighting knights.

I'm sure you've heard of the Loch Ness Monster. She's famous for ... being spotted.

There she is!

Where?

There!

The Loch Ness Monster is so famous she's even got her own nickname. They call her Nessie. Nessie, the Loch Ness Monster.

I've got a nickname too. Nessie calls me the Luckless Monster.

She calls me Luckless because I never seem to have any luck at all, but Luckless isn't my real name.

My real name is Flossie.

This is where we live.

It's a bit wild … a bit windy … a bit wet, but it's home to us. I love it here.

But it can be lonely.

I belong to the same family as Nessie. I live in the same loch as Nessie. I swim in the same water. I hunt for the same fish. But we do have our differences.

For instance, the Loch Ness Monster is huge and scary.

But I'm a bit on the small side. Sometimes Nessie calls me Titch or Shrimp.

The Loch Ness Monster swims down to the dark depths of the loch.

But I'm a bit scared of the dark. Sometimes Nessie calls me Scaredy Cat.

The Loch Ness Monster swims swift and sure.

But I'm not all that keen on water.

I don't like the cold and wet. I don't like the high waves. I don't like the deep pools and I HATE the whirlpool.

This is the whirlpool.

It goes round and round and round, and whatever is in the whirlpool goes round and round with it.

Nessie LOVES it. 'Wheee!' she yells.

'Yeeeeeeeeh!' she yells, and, 'Come and have a go if you think you're brave enough!'

I had a go once. I HATED it. The water went up my nose, I couldn't see anything and I felt dizzy and sick.

'You're scared!' Nessie teased. 'You're frightened!'

But I wasn't frightened.

I was TERRIFIED!

Nessie called me a landlubber, a chicken.

Nessie calls me lots of names: Titch! Scaredy cat! Cry baby!

To tell you the truth, Nessie is a bit of a bully. But *nothing* Nessie can do would make me get back in that whirlpool again.

Never!

2

No one cares about YOU!

You probably know that the Loch Ness Monster (or Nessie for short) is good at hiding. We monsters have learned the art of camouflage. This means we can hide by changing our colour or making ourselves look like other things.

If someone spots Nessie, she changes.

People who make films, and people who write for newspapers and magazines, are always trying to spot Nessie. They want to take her photo. They want to make a film about her. They want her to be in their newspapers or magazines.

She's famous. She's a celebrity. Everyone tries to spot Nessie.

But nobody has ever tried to spot *me*.

I WANT to be spotted. I want to be noticed. I want to be made a fuss of. But no matter what I do, *nobody* notices me at all.

That's why Nessie calls me the Luckless Monster. 'No one *knows* you exist. No one *cares* if you exist!' she says.

'*Na na na na na,*' Nessie sings.
No one tries to take photos of you!
No one talks about you.
No one cares about YOU at all.'

It's true. I don't have any *real*
friends.

There's Nessie of course – but she
only talks to me when she feels like it.
She only plays with me when she feels
like playing. So I'm lonely, and that's
why I think Nessie is right when she
calls me the Luckless Monster.

3

How do you find a friend?

One day, I woke up and I said to myself,
'Enough is enough. Today is the day I
will find a real friend, a good friend.
Nessie doesn't care if she has a friend,
but *I* do.'

I want someone who cares for me. I
want someone who can see the real me.

But how do you find a friend?

What exactly *is* a friend?

I thought about this for a long, long time. I even asked Nessie.

'What exactly *is* a friend?' I asked.

'A friend is someone who is like you, just like you,' she said. 'But no one is like us, so we CAN'T have friends. Better just to settle for scaring people.'

Then she gave a roar that sent me skittering away.

'It works for me,' she grinned. 'I *love* scaring people!'

But I didn't give up. I was determined to find a friend.

I asked all the animals I met, 'Please be my friend.'

This is what they said:

Miaou! No! You're too wet. Go away!

No, you are too big!

They thought I was too big, too wet, too scary looking and too fishy smelling.

Then I asked some children and this is what they said:

The grown ups said, 'Don't be silly. There are no such things as monsters. That's just a shadow. Come along, now. Hurry up.'

People were either scared of me – or they didn't believe in me.

It was hopeless. So I sulked. I'm very good at sulking. I can do it for ages.

I stayed perfectly still, crossed my arms, drooped my bottom lip and got ready for a HUGE sulk. I was just getting into it, when I heard a noise.

A group of children were going up to
a little girl. They were saying things
that sounded very familiar to me.

The girl was crying and she was
wearing glasses – but not for long.
The other children took her glasses
and started to pass them to each other.

Each time she tried to grab them back they threw them to someone else. They were throwing faster and faster and harder and harder until –

SPLASH! The glasses landed in the water.

They were light and plastic. So they bobbed about on the surface. Then they drifted in little circles.

The girl cried, 'Oh! No!'

Some of the children said, 'Ha ha!'

Some said, 'Oh, no! Sorry.'

Then all of the children went away, except for the girl, who stood peering at her glasses in the water.

First she tried reaching for them, but they were too far out.

Then she tried to hook them with a branch, but that didn't work. The glasses drifted further and further out.

Then the girl took a deep breath, and waded in after them. They were going towards the whirlpool.

That's when she should have given up – but on she went and … you can guess what happened next.

'Aaagh!' screamed the girl as she slipped and her head went under the water.

'AAAGH!' she cried out again, and down she went for the second time.

Well, I had no choice. A monster's got to do what a monster's got to do!

I grabbed her and kept her head out of the water.

Then off we went.

First we swirled,
then we whirled.

Then we swooshed
and we whooshed.

Funnily enough,
after a while …
… we almost started
to enjoy it.

At last we landed in a soggy heap.

We were out of breath but safe and
sound and the girl was still holding onto
her glasses.

She put her glasses on and peered at me. It must have been the first time she had seen me clearly and she looked a little surprised.

'I know I look a little bit … different,' I apologised.

'That's what people say about me!' she said. 'They think *I'm* different!'

'Is that why those children were calling you names?' I asked.

She nodded.

'*I* get called some of those same names,' I said, sadly.

'My real name is Flossie,' I told her.

'My real name is Fran,' she said. Then she smiled a little smile and said, 'We should be friends! Will you be my friend?'

'But I'm too big! I'm too wet! I'm too weedy,' I said. 'I'm different, too.'

'We're *both* different,' Fran said. 'So, in a way ... we're both the same!'

She went on, 'I like you. You're kind and you're friendly. *That's* what makes a friend for me.'

So we decided to be friends.

4

Can you see me?

Just then, the other children came
rushing up to Fran.

Quick as quick, I made myself look
like a very handsome tree. Well, I don't
want them screaming and running
away or calling me names, do I?

The other children ran up to my new
friend.

Sometimes I can hide myself just *too* well. But I don't mind.

Now, Fran and I often play together. We swim. We play tig and tag and hide and seek and skipping and football. I help her – and she helps me.

Yes, she's taught me to look at things differently.

30

Fran has lots of friends now but she's still *my* friend too.

I'm often around. But not everyone can spot me.

It takes a real friend to see me.

Can you?

About the author

I like writing stories! The best
part (for me) is thinking up
the story. Sometimes, it's
something I see that gives me
the idea. Sometimes, it's
something I hear.
Sometimes, the idea just
pops up from nowhere.

    This story started by mistake.
I thought I heard someone talking about 'the
luckless monster'. In fact they were talking
about the Loch Ness Monster. I started to
wonder why a monster would feel unlucky –
and so the story began ...